Come to the Table

A GUIDE FOR FAMILIES TO RESTORE THE DINNER HOUR AND HAVE FUN AND INTERESTING CONVERSATIONS

Nancy A. Cannon and Nancy Hennessy Cooney

Sheed & Ward
Kansas City

Sheed & Ward™ is a service of National Catholic Reporter Publishing Company, Inc.

ISBN: 1-58051-029-9

Published by: Sheed & Ward
115 E. Armour Blvd.,
P.O. Box 419492
Kansas City, MO 64141-6492.

To order, call: (800)333-7373

This book is reprinted on recycled paper.

Cover design by Michelle Stellmacher.

www.natcath.com/sheedward

Comments from Families Who Tested Come to the Table

"Terrific idea and it works! This book fosters a culture. The family begins to create its own meaning in the home rather than depend on the words and images of the media that would shape our thinking. . . . Our best sessions were when our 9-year-old Catherine was the leader."

Michael Warren, Ph.D. (2 children)
St. John's University, NY

"We began our dinner with our daughter thinking that 'Silent Night' was stupid--too elementary! After a few minutes of discussion, everyone decided to try it. We all had a great time with many wonderful comments being passed to each other. Even our dog, Obie, had four put under his dish. . . . We need this book as a family and a society . . . we do get in a rut in our family."

The Froze Family (2 children)
Bayside, WI

"I liked it when one of the children facilitated the discussion. It equalized the discussion . . . using the sage leaves at the end was a nice touch and the children seemed to enjoy that."

Tate/McHugh Family (4 children)
Philadelphia, PA

"I love the idea of the book. Even these brief experiences helped our family. . . .There is a hunger for this kind of communication. . . . We liked 'Baby Crab' best."

Bachhuber/ Maitlin Family (1 child)
St. Paul, MN

"Our experience was that the 'Jimjam' topic prompted much more spontaneous answers that were more feeling driven. We had a lot of fun talking about each others' answers and helping each other come up with additional answers."

DeJong Family (2 children)
Mequon, WI

Contents

A Special Thanks to . . .

Our families: Tom, Rachel, Niall, and Rory Cannon and Chuck, Katherine, and Stephen Cooney--for their love, encouragement and assistance.

Also thank you to the following families of: Jim and Patty DeJong, Dan Bachhuber and Todd Maitlin, Patrick and Marilyn Froze, Michael Warren and Connie Loose, Maureen Tate and Jerry McHugh and to Julie McLure, Florence, Marquez, Ileana Metamoros, Mustafa Kerem Gursu, Adam Singer, Chuck Gloor, Jean Marie Heisberger, *and* many thanks to Bob Heyer and all the staff at Sheed & Ward.

We are planning *Come to the Table II.* If you or your children have any suggestions, stories, pictures, ideas, or anecdotes for us to include in our next book, please send them along. (Make sure you list all sources and put names and addresses on submissions.) We are also very interested in hearing your response to this book: how did it work with your family, your most successful topics, favorite topics of the kids, parents, etc.

Both of us are experienced public speakers and workshop leaders. If you would like to contact us for your group, church, PTA, or club, you can reach us at:

E-mail: Com2Table@aol.com

OR

You can write to us at: Come to the Table
P.O. Box 11503
Milwaukee, WI 53211-0503

Thank you and keep talking,
Nancy & Nancy

Acknowledgements

Thank you to the following for permission to reprint material. We have tried to find all rights holders and to receive clear reprint permissions. This was a difficult process. If any required acknowledgements have been omitted, it was not purposeful. If notified, we will be pleased to correct any omissions in future editions.

Adapted from "Baytin: A Jordanian Village," by Abdulla Lutfiyya in *Through Middle Eastern Eyes,* edited by Robert P. Pearson.©1974 Praeger Press, Westport, CT.

Adapted from "A Place for Your Stuff," in *Brain Droppings,* by George Carlin. © 1997 Hyperion, NY.

Permisssion to quote from *The Way of Man* by Martin Buber. © 1995 Citadel Press, Carol Publishing Group, NY.

Permission to quote from an Easter Seal publication, © 1974 Easter Seal Society, Chicago, IL.

Permission to quote from *Peacemaking: Family Activities for Justice and Peace,* by Jacqueline Haessley. © 1980 Paulist Press, NJ.

Adapted with permission from "yin-yang" in *Encyclopaedia Brittannica,* 15th edition (1981), X:821.

Quoted from *The Oxford Book of Friendship,* chosen and edited by D.J. Enright and David Rawlinson. ©1991 Oxford University Press, NY.

By permission. From *Webster's Third New International ® Dictionary, Unabridged,* © 1993 by Merriam-Webster, Incorporated, Springfield, MA.

Permission to quote from *Keepers of the Night, Native American Stories and Nocturnal Activities for Children,* by Michael J. Caduto and Joseph Bruchac. © 1994 Fulcrum Publishing, Golden, CO.

Introduction

You and your family are invited to gather around a special place in your home that is designed to provide nourishment for the body, mind and heart: the dinner table.

Sharing a meal is a significant event that is rich with tradition and meaning throughout time and across many cultures. The family dinner table, which was once the focal point for all members of the household, is now too often a deserted place for solitary diners and a holding center for the clutter of books, papers, old mail, bills, school notes, etc. We need to restore our dinner tables to their sacred role of bringing families together at a place for sharing, listening, laughing, and reflecting.

Modern life has brought an abundance of ways to receive information and to connect with others all over the world. But in our most intimate worlds, particularly the ever important world between parents and children, are we talking more--or less? And what is that conversation like? Is it more often filled with parents correcting their children, reminding them how to behave, lecturing to them, cross-examining them about homework or friends? Is that what masquerades for conversation in most homes and during most dinner hours?

The purpose of this book is to provide a stimulant to our imaginations on how to communicate as a family at that rare time when we are all gathered for a common purpose: the sharing of food. *Come to the Table* was designed to stand up and find a place on your table and in your lives.

HOW TO USE THIS BOOK: We suggest you use it any way you can make it work for you and your family. For starters, there are fifty-two topics for family discussion--one for each week of the year. Most families are unable to eat together every night. But all families can make a commitment to dine together at least once a week. It is important to set goals that you can reach.

Even if you do eat together every day or several times a week, we suggest that you still only have **one night a week set aside for these special discussions**. For example, one of you could say, "If it's Tuesday, it must be *Come to the Table* day."

We suggest then that **one person read the topic and lead the discussion and that you rotate the leadership position.** In other words, you are all participants and you are all leaders. For once, let the monotonous ruts of "parent/child" that we all get stuck in evaporate for a short time. We are all human beings sharing this meal at this time in this place called home. Now we need to get to know each other as people with our own ideas, likes and dislikes, fears, dreams, and unique imaginations. You will be amazed at how this appeals to children.

The **discussion time** should be decided ahead, for example, **ten minutes** during dinner or ten minutes after dessert. The topic could be read before the food is passed and the discussions take place during dinner, or it could be read after dessert while everyone sits back, digests, and discusses. If you set

a time limit and stick to it, then family members will not begrudge the time asked of them. It will also help to keep it from being boring. **Remember: short is sweet . . . and hopefully successful**.

WHAT AGES ARE SUITABLE FOR THIS BOOK?

We think most adults are able to participate—as long as they follow the rules. Ah, the children? Well, each family will have to decide that for itself. We would never underestimate a child's potential and ability to discern and discuss. Also, most families have children of mixed ages, say, a ten-year-old and a four-year-old. Of course, you can start talking now and not wait for the four-year old to turn five or six. And if you think your teenagers will pooh-pooh this attempt at family communication, think again! We have found teenagers and early adolescents to be the most enthusiastic participants--as long as the adults try to follow the rules: rotate leadership, don't try to preach, accuse, teach, or lecture. We suspect that the stereotype of the silent, withdrawn, boy-are-my-parents-out-

of-it adolescents is inaccurate. They really just want a format where they can be respected and listened to! Try it. Surprise yourselves.

The topics that have been selected provide an interesting buffet. Some of them are serious, others are inspirational, and still others are simply fun and frothy and sweet and spicy. They contain all of the flavors, tastes, scents, and smells of the life of the mind and heart wanting to be expressed and heard. They are designed to be starting points for your individual and unique family's blend of ideas and opinions. Think of the topics as the appetizers to whet your palate before a meal and then think of all of your family members' thoughts and feelings swirling around as the main course. Dessert? Well, the delight in seeing your family strengthened and coming together in ways unknown to you all will be your "just desserts" and rewards.

RULES FOR DISCUSSION

1. No one is forced to participate, but all can be encouraged by being asked their opinions, feelings, or thoughts.

2. This is a special time for listening and sharing thoughts and feelings. It is not a time to correct table manners, bring up other problems (e.g., " Excuse me, did you take out the garbage yet?")

3. No outside interruptions will be attended to, e.g., the telephone is to be ignored and, in our opinion, should never be answered during dinnertime.

4. Everyone's feelings and thoughts are to be heard and respected. There can be no put-downs of ideas (e.g., "That's ridiculous.") or other unspoken signs of disapproval (snorting, derisive laughing, etc.).

5. We suggest that instead of Mom or Dad always being in charge, the responsibilities of reading the topic and leading the discussion are shared by all. Children feel more willing to participate when they see they are on equal footing. Even the youngest child can learn to lead discussions by calling on people as they raise their hands.

A FEW MORE REASONS WHY YOU SHOULD TRY *COME TO THE TABLE:*

We all desire closeness in our relationships, but we haven't learned how to create an environment for it to happen. We all want to have the kind of family that supports its members. However, our good intentions often fall by the wayside when we lean on outdated ways of interacting with each other (for example teasing, which often fails miserably in bringing us together but succeeds in mucking up relationships).

Silent dinner tables are another common problem. Our children desperately desire to know their parents as human beings and not just parents stuck in the role of acting as authority figures. Many parents want to talk to their kids but feel a chasm to cross whenever they attempt to do so. Too often, the communication consists of the parent asking a question and the child answering, (e.g., Parent: "What did you do in school today?" Child: "Nothing."). Then the parents give up complaining that the kids never talk to them or only grunt out one-word answers. Too often, parents think that they have to have all the answers. In *Come to the Table*, **we raise the questions.**

So don't give up. Keep talking, just change the format. Be creative. Approach things in a new way. Use this book to get you started. In no time at all, you will notice how loud and noisy and fun your dinner table will become. The air will be filled with chattering voices and clinking forks and the warm glow of hearts growing closer.

About the Authors:

Nancy A. Cannon has worked as a teacher, a family counselor, and a mental health consultant to schools and parent groups for the past twenty-eight years. She has a master's degree in counseling psychology. She is a public speaker and has lectured throughout the United States. She is especially well-known for her fun and humorous workshops on child rearing. She has three children and lives in Wisconsin with her family.

Nancy Hennessy Cooney is a parent, educator and author of books and articles for teens and adults in the areas of religious and sexuality education. She has master's degrees in theology and management. She has worked in religious education for the past thirty years. As a member of The Grail, an international women's movement, she serves on the leadership team of the Grail Women with Children Network. She lives in Milwaukee with her family.

1

Jimjams

When do you get the **jimjams**? Never heard of them? Okay, here are some hints as to **WHAT THE JIMJAMS ARE:**

HINT #1: Everyone gets them, but they are not contagious.

HINT #2: They come at different times for different people depending on the situation.

HINT #3: People feel them in different parts of their bodies: in the stomach, in the knees, in the throat, etc.

So **what are the jimjams?** Any guesses?

Answer: The *jimjams* are the nervous feelings you get. *Jimjams* are a state of nervousness. For example, some people say when they get up to talk in front of the class, they feel butterflies in their stomach. Well, now they can say they feel the *jimjams* in their stomachs.

So there are times we all feel nervous. Go around the table and ask each person to tell the times that they feel the *jimjams* and where in their bodies they feel them. (Start with Mom or Dad.)

So, now what can you do to make the *jimjams* go away? (Ask for ideas.)

> Has anyone ever tried taking three, slow breaths?

> Has anyone ever tried talking to them as friends? Do they help us?

> Does it help knowing that you're not alone and that the *jimjams* visit all of us at times?

Optional: Get paper and crayons and everyone draw them picture of what *jimjams* look like and where they come in their own bodies. Share the pictures and put them up on the fridge.

"Eat What You Please, But Wear What Pleases Others"

– Egyptian Proverb

Do you agree or disagree with this proverb? Why?

EATING:

1. Are we as a family happy with what we are currently eating during the day and at meals?   Why or why not?

2. What changes in eating have we gone through as individuals and as a family over the years?

WEARING:

1. Do you dress to please others? (Rate youself: Sometimes___Always___ Never___)

2. Are there times when you might need to dress to please others? Can you give an example?

3. Do you have any stories when what you were wearing got you into a funny or embarrassing situation?

4. Have you any suggestions to others in the family about what they might wear that pleases you?

Hospitality

*In a Jordanian village, everyone is expected to visit neighbors and relatives at their homes on religious holidays. Upon entering a house, the guests are expected to give it their blessing. The host shakes hands with each guest several times and leads them into the house where they are offered the best seats.

The host's duty is to make the guest feel comfortable and welcome. The host feels delighted and honored by the visit. The host gives the impression that there is no other work to do so as to spare the guests the feelings of imposing. The host offers coffee immediately and the guests accept because it would be an insult to the host to reject it. Later the guests will be served the very best food for as long as they remain.

Let's reflect

1. What are some of the rituals that your family uses for greeting and making guests feel welcome?

2. Are your family members good at acting as though they have nothing else to do so as to help the guests feel welcome?

3. Are some guests more welcome than others? Why?

4. What do you wish other family members would say (or not say) or do (or not do) when you have a guest to dinner or for a visit?

*From Abdulla Lutfiyya, "Baytin, A Jordanian Village," in *Through Middle Eastern Eyes.*

4

Stuff

The comedian *George Carlin has a routine in which he talks about Americans as obsessed with their "stuff." We buy backpacks, purses, CDs, comic books, makeup, baseball caps, clothes and more clothes, shoes, and on and on. We buy big houses and rent space in warehouses to store all the stuff. We build multicar garages to store the vehicles that drive us and our "stuff" around.

We buy guns and hire police and soldiers to protect our "stuff." Sometimes we clean out our "stuff" and give it away, only to find we still have more "stuff" than we ever need or use. Stuff! Is it taking over and multiplying all by itself? Is it the "Revenge of the Stuff?"

YIKES!!!

1. Do you think we have too much stuff, too little stuff, or just enough stuff?

2. What stuff do you love and could not live without? Name two.

3. What stuff do you know you could live without? Name two.

4. How do advertisements on TV work in trying to get us to buy their stuff?

5. How do the displays in stores entice us to buy?

6. What are good tips for resisting displays and advertisements?

*Adapted from "Brain Droppings," by George Carlin, in *A Place for Your Stuff* (New York: Hyperion, 1997), pp. 36-42.

You-neek

The famous Rabbi Zusya lectured to many, many people. They followed him to learn from him because he was so wise. Shortly before he died, he said, "In the world to come I shall not be asked: 'Why were you not Moses?' I shall be asked, 'Why were you not Zusya?'"

WHAT IN THE WORLD DOES THAT MEAN?

1. Do you ever wish that you were someone else? Parents tell first!

2. Are there messages in our lives that suggest we are not good enough as we are? What happens when these messages get inside us?

3. What would this family be like if everyone was the same, you know, same hair, same eyes, same body shape, same voice, same personality, same ideas, same likes and dislikes? Imagine it . . . well?

4. Now imagine you going to school or work and everyone is the same: same color of skin, same body type, same abilities, same interests, same personalities. There are no more problems caused by comparing yourself to anyone else--because you are all the same. Is that a relief?

What does the title of this page mean? Do you really appreciate the you in "unique"?

FUN TIP: The next time we start comparing ourselves to someone else, ask ourselves: "*WHY ARE YOU NOT ZUSYA?*"

Martin Buber, *The Way of Man*, p. 18.

6

Stop Reminding and Get Creative

Parents, are you tired of nagging your children?

Children, are you tired of your parents bugging you?

Well, it sure would be a nice and easy world if we were all perfect and did everything we were supposed to in just the right way. **BUT IT ISN'T AND IT NEVER WILL BE--SO SNAP OUT OF IT!**

If we can't change the fact that parents will act like parents and kids will act like kids, maybe we can remind each other to try some new and fun ways of living together.

The ol' Augean stable message.
Mom discovers child's messy room says,

"Honey, your room looks like the *Augean stable.*"

(A long time ago in Greece there was a king, King Augeas. He was not a clean dude. He had a huge stable with many, many animals living in it. Now this particular stable had not been cleaned in thirty years! Man, the smell alone! Anyway, it was up to Hercules to take care of this problem and clean that stable!)

Mom repeats: "Honey, your room looks like the *Augean stable . . .* and you have till noon to find Hercules!"

Where are the Augean stables in your house?

7

Scars

"People stare at me a lot and wonder why that happened to that certain person. I ask myself that a lot sometimes, too . . . I don't think anybody's ugly. I think that something ugly always has something beautiful in it" (Easter Seal Youth).

HMMM . . . THINGS TO THINK ABOUT

1. Have you ever known someone who had a facial scar or some other disfigurement? How did you treat the person?

2. What about your own *visible or invisible* scars? Most people get hurt one way or another when they are growing up. How do you deal with your hurts?

3. Have you ever met someone considered beautiful our culture, who turned out to be mean or ugly inside?

4. Have you ever met somebody considered ugly by our culture who turned out to be a beautiful person inside?

8

Nom De Plume

Sometimes people like to use disguises. At Halloween, you get to dress up and ring doorbells and ask people for candy. So disguises can be fun. Sometimes disguises are used to hide under. For example, writers often make up a **Nom De Plume**, which is French for "name of the pen" or, as we know today, a **Pen Name.** A **Nom De Plume** allows a writer to feel free to write different kinds of stories and not get boxed into writing just one kind of story.

Noms De Plume can be fun and useful in your family. *First,* everyone make up a *Nom De Plume.* Haven't you always wanted to give yourself a new name? It can be just one name, or initials, or whatever! Take a few minutes to think up a new name, then share it with everyone.

Now, you ask, how can *Noms de Plume* be helpful in the everyday life of the family?

Well, here is just *one way:* You know how sometimes you do things that you don't like to admit? Like, "who ate all of the icing off the cake?" or "Who didn't put out some more toilet paper?" Well, now you can "fess up" before the detectives get hot on your trail and get you in trouble. Now you say, "I know who did it!" and use your *Nom De Plume*! Or you can tell on the culprit by using his/her *Nom De Plume.*

Suggestions

1. Write down and put on the fridge the list of *Noms de Plume* for each member of the family.

2. Call each member by the *Nom De Plume* throughout dinner for one night.

9

Celebrations

Preparation: Balloons by each person's chair.

When you hear the word *celebration,* what comes to your mind? (Take time for people's responses.)

What makes *celebrations* special? (Go around and ask for their thoughts.)

List the ways that we, as a family, *celebrate.* (You can write them down if you wish.)

Something to think about

*"Celebration has lost its simplicity and spontaneity. Families and groups no longer respond with their own creativity to significant events in their lives. Rather celebration has been replaced with 'Sell-abration' . . . Buy, buy, buy becomes their common chant . . . In our consumer-oriented society, gift-giving of *presents* replaces the long established practice of giving *presence.*"

What do you think of that quote?

As a family, do you think *we celebrate enough?*

As a family, would you like *to celebrate* in new ways? Such as?

Optional: Plan a new celebration sometime within the next few weeks, e.g., have you ever celebrated the moon rising? (check your calendar), celebrated the Solstice?, celebrated the new ways we share and talk as a family?, etc. Find a time and place when all family members are available, then make a list of who will select the music, the activities, etc.

Peacemaking: Family Activities for Justice and Peace, by Jacqueline Haessly.

10

Skin Hunger

Matt, age two, fell and scratched his finger on the fence and let out a yell. He ran to his dad, who picked him up, gave him a big hug, and was heading inside to the medicine cabinet when Matt held the finger to his dad's lips and said:

"Give it a kiss, Dad."

His dad did as he was told. "Here you are, Matt, does it feel any better?"

"Yeah," he said, "I'll need a Band-Aid, too."

WHAT WAS THE MEDICINE that made Matt feel better?

Scientists tell us that touch is absolutely necessary to our growth. We all have **"SKIN HUNGER." SKIN HUNGER** is the strong need to be touched or held. Sometimes words alone can't help us feel better. But a touch--a hug, a kiss, a pat--can do more for us than anything else when we are hurting or feeling lost.

Family medical exam

1. Who can remember a time when a hug from a family member meant a great deal?

2. Name a time you felt *skin hunger.*

3. When was the last time you hugged someone in your family?

4. When are the times you feel you need to be touched, held, or hugged the most? (Parents go first.)

JUST FOR FUN

What kind of a *hugger* are you?

Who is a *bear* hugger? Describe a bear hugger or give a bear hug to the person next to you.

Who is a *patter*? Show us.

Who is a *squeezer*? Do a squeeze hug.

Any other kinds of huggers?

11

Signals & Key Words

THE BABY CRAB AND HER MOTHER

– Adapted from Aesop

One day a mother crab and her little crab went for a walk along the beach. They were enjoying the ocean breeze and the soft warm sand under their claws. "Oh, honey," the mother crab said, "don't walk so cookedly." "Yes, Mamma." The little crab replied and sighed. They continued walking along and the mother crab again spoke, "Now, honey, look again how you walk--so crookedly. Don't do that." "Yes, Mamma." The little crab sighed again, "but, Mamma, I walk just like you do. You taught me how to walk. So if you want me to walk straight, you must do so, too. I will do whatever you do."

HMM. . . .

1. There is an old phrase that fits the moral of this story perfectly. Anyone know what it is? (Wait for answers. . . ."Do as I say, not as I do.")

2. Discuss the things that adults tell children not to do, but children watch them do those things.

3. Do older children set good examples for their younger brothers and sisters? Do younger children imitate the way they are treated? Any examples?

HOW TO USE SIGNALS

Some families like to use a *SIGNAL OR SPECIAL WORD* that will remind them to change some of their behaviors. For example, when someone sets a bad example, you could say **"CRAB"** instead of fighting or arguing or reminding.

12

Yin-Yang

There is in Chinese thought the wonderful idea of *two forces* that can be found everywhere . . . in people, in the world, and in all aspects of life. These two forces are called *YIN-YANG.*

Yin is the female life force and is found in the Earth and in even numbers, and in valleys and streams, and is expressed in the color orange, and the tiger and a broken line.

Yang is the male life force and found in the sky, and in odd numbers, and in the mountains, and is expressed in the color azure and an unbroken line.

*The two forces, yin-yang, first came from the Supreme Ultimate, or T'ai Chi. They act upon each other, with one increasing and then the other decreasing. They represent the process of the universe. *When yin-yang are in harmony, they are shown as the light and dark halves of a circle.*

FOOD FOR THOUGHT

1. Do you think we all have a balance within us of male and female or yin-yang?

2. Are boys and men afraid of their yin or female sides? Are girls and women afraid of their male or yang sides?

3. Have you ever heard boys or men say to other males, "You play like a girl." Are they comparing them to Olympic champions like Jackie Joyner Kersee or Bonnie Blair? Is it a compliment?

4. What about when someone says a woman is "too aggressive"? Can a woman be feminine and aggressive? Can a boy be sensitive and strong?

6. What does it mean to be "all boy or all girl?"

7. Is there a way to be boy or girl, or man or woman that is already marked out for us? Or do each of us create our own way of being male and female?

13

Do We Ever Get Stuck?

Do we ever get stuck in our bad habits? It's not easy to change and do things differently.

So tonight let's do a little experiment:

LET'S ALL EAT BACKWARDS!!!
OK, it sounds weird, but let's just try. Here is how it works:

If you usually eat with your right hand, tonight, eat with your *left* hand and vice versa. Yes, throughout the whole meal! All right, everyone switch forks to the *other* hand. Ready, set, cut, chop, lift. . . . No cheating. . . . throughout the whole meal . . . even dessert, and wiping your mouth with the napkin . . . other hand . . . GO!

AFTER DINNER
Well, how was it? Hard or easy? Awkward or smooth?

What does this little experiment show about habits?

A LITTLE SUGGESTION
The next time someone (say Mom or Dad) keeps acting in a way that needs to be changed, just say, *"I think it's time you start eating again with your other hand."*

14

Pals, Buddies & Chums

*"We have as many sides to our character as we have friends to show them to . . . I find myself witty with one friend, large and magnanimous with another, petulant and stingy with another, wise and grave with another, and utterly frivolous with another. . . . We let ourselves out piecemeal it seems, so that only with a host of varied friends can we express ourselves to the fullest."

> – Randolph Bourne,
> "The Excitement of Friendship," 1912

1. Give examples of friends who draw out different qualities in you.

2. For many young people, some of the hardest times in keeping friends, losing friends, or the re-arranging of friends is during the school years, especially middle and high school. Can anyone give examples of this? (Parents first.) Is there a purpose in all of this re-arranging?

Write a Recipe for Friendship

1. What are some of the different ways to *make a friend or to start up a friendship*?

2. List some of the *qualities*, or things, that you like to see or have *in a friend*.

The Shipwreck of a Friendship

1. List some of the things that cause disaster and breakup friendships.

2. Can some friendships be toxic, i.e., harmful like poison. Give examples.

The Oxford Book of Friendship, by D.J. Enright and David Rawlinson (New York: Oxford University Press, 1991), p. 12.

15

Swamps

There is a place that we can visit that is wet and spongy and filled with sludge. Once we go into this place, it is very easy for us to get swallowed up and sink deeper and deeper into it. As we sink deeper and deeper into it, we don't know how to get out. We only know how unhappy we are, and we feel more and more miserable. This place is the swamp in our minds. We sink into it every time we say negative things.

Some examples of swamps

"I hate school. It is stupid and boring and I'll never use this stuff anyway."

"I'll never be able to do it. So why bother wasting my time trying?"

Do these statements give someone permission to give up? Or are they just excuses?

Other words for swamps: BAD ATTITUDE . . . NEGATIVE THINKING

SOMETIMES **people try to pull others into their swamps.**

1. Can you think of how they do that?

2. Are "dissing" others, put downs, and bullying comments ways of trying to pull others into their swamps?

3. How about "teasing" comments that make fun of people's clothes, hair, learning styles, good grades, etc.? How does the person who is teased feel after the teasing?

Go around the table and ask each person to share one time they were in a swamp.

Next week, discuss the next topic--*"The Magic Light Switch."*

16

The Magic Light Switch

Have you ever been to a basketball game or a football game or even a game in your gym class when your team was losing? Your team was behind and had been behind for most of the time. Then all of a sudden, someone on your team made a basket or caught the ball and scored!!! Suddenly, *the momentum had changed!* Now you and your team became all fired up and started to play differently and the score reflected that change! You were close to winning or actually were winning! What a great feeling of triumph and hope!

SOMEONE HAD TURNED ON THE MAGIC LIGHT SWITCH!

Yes, the magic light switch. You can't see it. But it's there . . . within you. It is a switch that you can turn on when you decide to. *YOU TURN IT ON AND OFF WITH YOUR MIND AND YOUR ATTITUDE*. **And then it has a *powerful* effect!**

SOME PEOPLE USE THE MAGIC LIGHT SWITCH TO GET OUT OF THEIR SWAMPS.

1. Can you think of a time you turned on your magic light switch and got out of your swamp? (Parents first.)

2. How did you feel when you got out of the swamp, which was heavy and pulling you down, and then switched on your magic light switch? (Use adjectives to describe.)

3. Do other people *really* have the power to put you into a swamp by things they say? Or do you put yourself there by letting the things they say get to you? So who has the power?

4. Do you agree that people can have *a change of heart in a moment* **IF** they make up their minds to?

OPTIONAL

Each family member draws and colors a picture of their magic light switch. Is it a button? A spring? A slinky? Or maybe it is invisible and is just a group of colors? Use your imaginations!

17

Table fire . . . Campfire

Preparation: A candle or a group of candles

BEFORE DINNER

Place a lighted candle or group of several candles in the center of the table and turn out all the lights in the house. Everyone should sit down and before passing food, ask all family members to look at the fire in the center of the table.

Let's imagine it is our campfire and it is a million years ago. We are one of the early peoples on earth. We gather here in our cave, and it is very dark and really cold. A herd of woolly mammoths can be heard stampeding on the plain just outside our cave. The only warmth and light is in here around this little fire.

PASS THE FOOD IN SILENCE AND THINK

What kinds of things do you think our early ancestors worried about? After the food is passed, ask for ideas.

During dinner read and discuss

Some scientists think that the campfire was a very important part of human evolution because it gave people a place to talk after a hard day's search for food. People survived and found better ways of food gathering because they listened and learned from the stories they told to one another.

As they stared into the fire, they could also relax and unwind from a treacherous day of running for their lives from animals three times their size. With the light from the fire projecting their shadows onto the cave walls, they even began to entertain each other with scary or funny stories of their dangerous encounters in the wilds.

How do you feel sitting in the darkness around the fire? Cold? Scared? Warm? As a family, think about whether you want to have more table fires and when, e.g., after a fight or disagreement?

18

Sage

Preparation: A few leaves from the herb *sage*

Do you know what the word *SAGE* means? *According to Webster's Dictionary*, a sage is "one who is wise . . . rich in experience and sound in judgment." It defines wisdom as having the "ability to discern inner qualities and essential relationships."

Is there a difference between being smart and being wise? What do you think?

When you think of someone who is smart, who comes to mind? If you think of someone who is wise, who do you think of?

THINGS TO PONDER
1. Remembering the people that you listed as smart and as wise, who has the ability to see the inner qualities? Give examples of how they see inner qualities.

2. What are the "not important" things in relationships between family members and between friends?

3. Is wisdom something you want to have? Would your life and your decisions be better if you had wisdom or does it not matter just as long as you are smart?

PASS AROUND THE SAGE
Sage is also an herb that is used in flavoring foods and as a tonic, i.e., something to give you zip. Pass around the leaves of the sage plant. Let everyone take one leaf and smell it. Now, rub the leaf on your fingers and smell. How is the lingering smell of the sage on your fingertips like wisdom that floats into everyday life giving it a lift?

*Webster's Third New International Dictionary, Unabridged, Editor-in-Chief, Philip Babcock Grove, Ph.D, p.1999, G. & C. Merriam Company, Springfield, Massachusetts, 1971.

19

Funniest Home Stories

Remember when? That was so-o-o funny or the time that Dad . . . and the look on Mom's face. . . Hilarious!!! Yup, tonight we are going to conjure up all those sidesplitting times that cracked us up.

So . . . **as the food is passed**, everyone is asked to remember something funny that happened in this family, or to this family, or with a family member and retell the whole thing!!!

Now, **after the food is passed**, the leader starts with a hilarious account of the time when and each family member follows with their choice of fabulously funny moments in the life of the _____ family.

VARIATION

1. Set up the videotape on a tripod and let 'em roll! Or record the stories on a boom box. Anyway, save it and play the tape back five years from now or on birthdays and see how much everyone has changed!

2. Type up the stories and print out copies as little booklets. Family members can decorate, add pictures or drawings at the next family night.

20

The Silent Night

Please read before dinner:

E-mail should be left on the computer. Tonight is the night to send H-MAIL.

During dinner tonight, there is to be NO TALKING . . . none . . . not even a whisper . . . only the sounds of food being passed and brains clicking. (OK, maybe a few giggles are permitted.)

Have strips of paper and a pencil by each person's plate during the dinner . . . all eat silently . . . look at each other . . . no, ponder each other . . . and think of a short, fun, serious, sweet WHATEVER.

H-MAIL: THAT STANDS FOR *HEART MAIL* to write . . . fold . . . and slip next to the plate of each family member. . . . (yeah, getting up and walking around the table is permitted tonight and maybe more giggling).

After dinner . . . everyone . . . SILENTLY . . . reads all of the H-MAIL . . . and then . . . each person is to go and hug each other . . . SAYING the only words PERMITTED:

Thank you and I love you.

21

Heroes, Heroines and Role Models

What would it be like to have all the money you ever needed and more? Lots more. Tons more. What if you belonged to one of the richest families in America, like William Larimar Mellon, Jr. As in oil, Gulf Oil? What would you do with all of your money? Well, here is what William Mellon, Jr. did:

He was born into money, servants, yachts, limos, big houses, huge allowances--supposedly all the stuff some people dream about spend a lot of time and energy trying to get. But one day Mr. Mellon, Jr., read about Albert Schweitzer, who was a doctor devoted to helping the sick in a faraway spot in Africa. He began to write to Dr. Schweitzer. Suddenly Mr. Mellon, Jr. decided to go to medical school and became a doctor at the age of forty-four! His wife went and studied to be a lab technician! You see, they had a plan. They moved to Haiti, a very poor country, and took some of their money and built a two-million-dollar hospital and worked there for the rest of their lives!

SO WHAT DO YOU THINK OF THAT? (and other thoughts)

1. Why did Mr. Mellon, Jr. and Mrs. Mellon leave a life that everyone is trying to get--for a life that hardly anybody wants?

2. How do you think Mr. and Mrs. Mellon, Jr., would finish this sentence: "Happiness lies in. . ."

3. Now go around your table and ask each person to finish this sentence: "Happiness lies in . . ."

22

What's in a Name?

Why were you given your name? Is there a story behind it? What is it? What does your name mean? (You may need a book of names to look up their meanings.)

Why do we give each other names? Why not call each other numbers? Or adjectives? Like August girl, or June boy, or Monday or Eleven A.M. (time of birth).

Listen to how Native Americans are named

*"Children of Native North American families are given different names as they grow older and reach important times of passage in their lives. In many cultures the *birth name* traditionally refers to a child's order of birth. Among the Santee Dakota, for example, a child may be called *Chaskay* (first-born son) or *Wenonah* (first-born daughter).

Among the Dakotas, *honor* or *public names* are usually given by the clan leader once the child can walk. This is an occasion for a great feast and celebration around a communal fire. . . . A child who becomes distinguished in an honorable way later in life--because of a feat of endurance, strength, courage or compassion--may be awarded a *deed name* after a bird or other animal or even one of the elements."

Think about That

1. Each family member "choose a new name for yourself based on a plant, animal or element in nature that you feel close to and which you feel fits your character."* Write it down on *one side* of a *folded* 5x7 card. Take turns telling each other why you chose the name.

2. Keep these cards on the table at each person's place all week.

Keepers of the Night: Native American Stories and Nocturnal Activities for Children, by Michael J. Caduto and Joseph Bruchac (Golden, Colo: Fulcrum, 1994), pp. 102-3.

23

Sacred Words

READ AND DISCUSS DURING DINNER

Have you ever thought about words? Yes, just words. You can't see or touch them when they are spoken, but only when they are silent and written. How can such invisible and abstract things be so powerful?

Words can do strange things to us. They can make us mad, or they can make us cry and feel sad. Or they can be filled with beauty and pictures of loveliness that can make us swoon and feel loved. Words. You put that collection of little symbols called letters in a certain arrangement and they move people upon hearing them to go to war or to do great acts of compassion. Wow! Words have "wow" power!

Some words become special to each of us. Sometimes we like to just hear the sound of them, like jabberwocky, jimjams, fuzzy, gossamer, sassafras, celestial, starry, etc. And some words are *SACRED*.

A *SACRED* word is one that is special and is filled with great meaning, tenderness, or holiness to us.

1. What are some of your favorite words--the ones that you like to hear and the ones that you like to feel tumbling around in your mouth?

2. What are some of your *SACRED* words? Tell why they are sacred to you or have each other guess why you like them.

AFTER DINNER

Take a few minutes to write down on one piece of paper a collection of your family's FUN WORDS. On another piece of paper, write down a collection of your family's SACRED WORDS. Hang these papers on the fridge for a few weeks for everyone to think about or to add to.

24

How to Be a Really Together Person

There is a lot to be learned from stories. Here is one from the Jewish tradition:

*There is a Judaic legend about Nittai, a Jewish gatherer of books, and a camel dealer. Nittai prepared to go for a trip one day and sent his servant to buy a camel and a saddle. The servant returned and when the saddle was removed from the camel, a fortune in rare diamonds was discovered hidden in a pouch. Nittai sent the diamonds back to the camel dealer with the message: "I bought a camel and a saddle, but not these jewels."

The grateful camel dealer came to thank Nittai. "Had you kept the diamonds," he said, "I could not have brought you to court."

"That is true," said Nittai, "But had I kept them, I would have lost my integrity. One can enter the Heavenly Kingdom without diamonds, but not without honesty."

"I have heard about this 'Heavenly Kingdom,'" said the camel dealer. "How does one get there?"

"First, my son, Heaven is neither 'up' nor 'down,' but in out hearts," said Nittai. "The way to reach it is through good deeds; and the best road of all is through charity.

So what do you think?

1. Nittai gave the diamonds back because he was worried about losing his integrity. What if you were Nittai, and you secretly *kept* the diamonds. How would you feel inside?

2. How does the title at the top of the page relate to this discussion?

What The Great Religions Believe, by Joseph Gaer, from New American Library.

25

Ouch, That Hurts

CAN YOU REMEMBER WHEN?

When was the last time you showed some special thing that you made to a family member (like a poem, a joke, a picture, a story?)

How did you feel right before you showed it to them?

How did you feel after you showed it to them?

When was the last time you cried in front of a family member? (Parents first.) How did those family members respond to you while you were crying?

All these actions make a person *vulnerable or "able to be wounded."*

Sometimes people who are closest to us "wound" us with words like:

"Where did you get THAT ugly shirt?"

"Stop crying. Don't act like a baby. It's not that big of a deal."

"Sorry I missed your performance (or game). I got stuck at work."

"Leave me alone. It's none of your business."

1. We don't like to let people know that they have hurt us. Yet how can we support each other if we don't let people know when we have been hurt?

2. What takes more courage: staying "cool" or "hard" or showing our wounds?

Time to decide: As a family, do we want to be able to be open to each other?

TIPS FOR SENDING MESSAGES WHEN YOU HAVE BEEN HURT

Tip 1: "OUCH!" is a good response when someone says something hurtful.

Tip 2: "Thanks, I needed that" tells a person that a touch or nice words made you feel better.

26

What Did You Say?

Scientists discovered that babies are able to make all the sounds that are needed for any languages in the world. This is why very young children can easily learn other languages. Don't you wish we could still do this?

Do you know kids who can speak more than one language?

What are some of the different languages you hear spoken at school, at work, or on the radio or TV?

HOW TO MAKE YOUR TABLE AN INTERNATIONAL ONE:

Tonight and during the week, try using some of these phrases during dinner for fun:

IS SOMETHING BURNING? (Spanish)

¿Se esta quemando algo?

(Seh sstah kemando all go?)

IT WAS A DELICIOUS MEAL. (Turkish)

Ellerinize saglik

(El ae ree knee zeh   sal look)

THANK YOU. (Crow – Native American)

Ahoó

(A hoe oh)

27

A Taste of Music

Leader's Preparation: Before tonight's meal, the leader is to ask every family member to bring to the table one of their favorite pieces of music to listen to during dinner. It can be a tape or CD, or it can be played on an instrument. The leader is responsible to have the CD player or boom box ready for use at the table.

AFTER EVERYONE IS SITTING AND BEFORE PASSING FOOD

Please read:

*"Songs are thoughts, sung out with the breath when people are moved by great forces and ordinary speech no longer suffices" (Orpingalik).

"Music and rhythm find their way into the secret places of the soul" (Plato).

Who would like to start with one of their favorite pieces of music and tell us why they like it, or how it finds its "way into the secret places of the soul"?

REMEMBER: NO CRITICIZING. Try to listen to the music through the ears of the other.

Play the music and start eating and when it is over ask how the others feel about it.

The leader plays each person's selection of music for the family to hear, asks why they like it, and then solicits reactions to each piece.

*The Netsilik Eskimos, from the book *Eskimo Songs and Stories.*

28

How Do We Learn to Hate?

Why do some children grow up to hate people who are a different color or have a different religion? Were they born that way? Where did they learn it? (Take time to discuss.)

Do you know people who hate others because they have "more"--more clothes, more money, more status, more friends, etc.?

DO WE HAVE ANY RESPONSIBILITY TO END HATRED?

Respond to the following examples

1. You are standing with a small group of people and someone uses a derisive name for a person of color. What would you do or say?

2. At a family gathering, a relative says an insensitive and derisive remark about a gay woman whom you know. What would you do or say?

3. A good friend of yours puts down a group of religious people for their "backward ways." What would you do or say?

Finally, would you admire someone who spoke up in a positive way in these situations? How would they seem to you--weak or strong?

What is the best antidote to hatred? An antidote is something that relieves or stops the poison. What is your antidote? Words? Gestures? Remembering something else like going outside and looking up at the sky?

29

What Would the World Be Like If . . .

There were NO ANIMALS????

Imagine your home, your outdoor area, your entire community silent. No birds, no ducks, no deer tracks in the snow, no dogs barking, no dogs walking, no fish, no lizards, no squirrels digging in your garden, no rabbits hopping, no owls hooting . . . nothing except humans.

Well? How would you like that?

Read how other people view animals:

*"In the Iroquois Thanksgiving Prayer, a prayer to be spoken at the start of any gathering . . . reminds us that our Creator made it so that there should be animals of many kinds. Some of these animals would be companions to the people. Some would help us by allowing us to use their bodies to provide food and clothing for the people, but only as long as we respect them and give them thanks and take only what is needed for the people to survive. Never more and never with cruelty. The animals have their own families and nations, and we must recognize them. We must respect them as brothers and sisters. Without the animals, our human lives would indeed be hard and lonely on this earth. . . . This is what I want us to remember--to respect the animals, to greet and thank them and to keep them in our minds and hearts." – Joseph Bruchac

Do we take animals for granted? (That means do we forget about them and not stop to think about what they add to our lives?)

OPTIONAL: Write a letter to the animals, or write a prayer of thanksgiving for the animals and what they bring to our lives. Do it together or alone.

Native American Animal Stories. Told by Joseph Bruchac.

30

The Two Levels of Listening

Have you ever been upset and felt misunderstood? People could hear your words and could even repeat them, but something was missing.

Does this happen more often between children and adults or just between friends?

When people try to listen to each other, it is like the two floors, or levels, in a home or building. On the top floor, we hear the words. But we have to go down to the main floor to hear the *feelings.* For example, a child comes home and says, "I had a terrible day at school." What do most adults say? (Discuss.) Do the adults often ask questions, "What's the matter?" and try to solve the problem? Or do the adults often criticize, "I'm tired of hearing how you don't like school." Are the adults on the main floor, the floor, of feelings, when they respond like that? (Discuss.)

Now practice. Go around the table and read a sentence and have each person take a turn listening for the **feeling:**

1. I'm never riding on that school bus again.

2. You kids always leave your shoes right where I trip over them.

3. You had no right going in my room and taking my book.

4. I want to quit music lessons.

5. Why can't you get yourself up on time and out the door like everyone else?

For one week, practice **listening on both floors, words and feelings,** with your friends and family. See if it provides a new avenue to understand others and to get to know them better.

31

Secrets, Puzzles & Prudence

SECRETS

The Story of the Farmer and the Fox (Aesop).

One day a farmer woke up and went out to feed his chickens. He counted them and found another one missing! The farmer was furious! He knew it was the same fox--the one that snuck in at night and ran off with all of his chickens. He decided to get even with the fox and planned his revenge. That night, the farmer waited for the fox. When the fox came, he splashed gasoline on its tail and set it on fire. The fox ran crazily back and forth and then took off in the direction of the farmer's cornfield, which was ready for harvesting. As the fox ran through the field, the cornstalks caught fire. In a very short time, the entire field was burned up. The farmer lost his entire crop.

1. There is a secret message in this story of Aesop's. What do you think it is?

2. What does the saying "revenge is a two-edged sword" mean?

Next week, read the topic called *Secrets, Puzzles & Prudence*

32

Secrets, Puzzles & Prudence

The Story of the Goat and the Donkey
(Adapted from Aesop)

There was a goat who sat everyday and watched his owner give the donkey more food and special treats than he got. The goat grumbled to himself and was jealous. One day the goat couldn't stand it any more and trotted over to the donkey with a little plan. He said, "You work way too much around here. I've got a great idea for you. This afternoon when they come to make you carry those heavy bags, pretend to trip on a rock and fall down that hill. Then, you won't have to work!" The donkey liked the idea. He tried it, but it didn't go quite as planned. The donkey ended up breaking his leg and cutting himself. The owner sent for the doctor and the doctor said the donkey lost a lot of blood and would need plenty of meat in order to heal. The only animal on the farm was the goat, so they killed the goat and fed him to the donkey.

THE PUZZLE? LOOK FOR THE MISSING PIECE IN PRUDENCE:

PRUDENCE is defined as showing self-control, using caution and being shrewd or clever.

1. How could the goat have acted prudently?

2. When you plot to do harm to others, who often gets hurt?

Re-write or re-tell the story of the Farmer and the Fox (From *Secrets,* Puzzles & Prudence) and the Goat and the Donkey using prudence instead of revenge. Start with something like this: "So instead of the famer. . . ." or "Then the goat could have. . . ."

What are the secrets in using prudence?

Have you ever thought that a person who uses self-control is actually *very shrewd*?

33

Aunt Sue's Stories *

Is your family rich? Some say that a family's real wealth lies in the memories and stories of family members, such as grandparents, great-grandparents, aunts, and uncles. Langston Hughes was a great American poet who honored his Aunt Sue and her valuable gift to his family:

Aunt Sue has a head full of stories.
Aunt Sue has a whole heart full of stories.
Summer nights on the front porch
Aunt Sue cuddles a brown-faced child to her bosom
And tells him stories.
Black slaves
Working in the hot sun,
And black slaves
Walking in the dewy night,
And black slaves
Singing sorrow songs on the banks of a mighty river
Mingle themselves softly
In the flow of old Aunt Sue's voice,

Mingle themselves softly
In the dark shadows that cross and recross
Aunt Sue's stories
And the dark-faced child, listening,
Knows that Aunt Sue's stories are real stories.
He knows that Aunt Sue never got her stories
Out of any book at all,
But that they came
Right out of her own life.
The dark-faced child is quiet
Of a summer night
Listening to Aunt Sue's stories.

1. How important are the stories that come out of our lives, and not out of a book?

2. Videotape your family's elders telling their stories, or start to write them down.

*The Collected Poems of Langston Hughes, ed. Arnold Rampersad. (New York: Knopf, 1994), p. 23.

34

Small Change

Have you ever heard these phrases said around your house?

"A penny saved is a penny earned?"

"Turn off the electricity! It costs money, ya know!"

"Wait! Take that coupon off the cereal box. I can save $.50!"

A lot of these comments are talking small sums of money. Yet, **small sums of money** can add up to **big bucks**!

TIME OUT FOR A LITTLE TEST

Go around and ask each family member to answer the following question:

Where do you spend your *extra* money? You know, money left over from an allowance, or after the bills are paid, or the money you get for your birthday, etc. Have one person get paper and pencil and be the scribe. The leader reads the following categories. If you spend your extra money in one or more of these categories, raise your hand. Then the scribe writes down the names with each category: (1) clothes (2) movies and video rentals (3) hair products and cosmetics (4) savings or piggy bank (5) tapes and CDS (music) (6) charity (7) comics, baseball cards, collectibles (8) candy and snacks (9) other.

Okay, now read the list aloud. Who spends on clothes? Did anyone save money? Did anyone give to charity?

HMM . . .

Are there any "small changes" that you want to make?

How do you start a *nest egg?* (A nest egg is a savings plan.)

35

Jackpot

Right this way to the jackpot!

Were you ever at a carnival where there was a tall tower with a bell on top? A strong man or woman would come along, take a large hammer, and hit the base of the contraption to make a ball shoot up the tower and ring the bell at the top. Then the person would win a big stuffed animal as well as the admiration of the crowd.

We all have something like that bell in our brains. It is called the pleasure center. It is our "jackpot." We "hit it" whenever we do things like eating that give pleasure. It rewards us for doing what we need to do to live. When we eat food, we feel pleasure, when we make love we feel pleasure. Other activities like playing an instrument, solving problems, doing a good job, or creating something bring us pleasure too.

These are all ways "to hit the jackpot."

But maybe NOT THIS WAY to the jackpot . . .

Some people take drugs as a shortcut to the pleasure center. With the right amount of the right drug, they can predict that they will hit the "jackpot." They will feel a rush of pleasure far better and faster than that which comes from everyday activities. They know drugs always destroy brain cells, but to them health is not the issue--feeling good is.

Discuss ways we hit the **wrong** jackpot:

1. What drugs do people in your family take regularly? For what purpose?

2. Have you ever known anyone who took illegal drugs or abused alcohol? What effect did that addiction have on their lives and the lives of their families?

36

The Talk

READ ALOUD

Pat and Jacob were friends. One day Pat saw Jacob sighing.

"What's the matter?" Pat asked him.

"I just had to listen to my dad give me THE TALK."

"What's THE TALK?" Pat asked.

"You know--THE TALK. The talk about how babies are made. You know--sex!"

"Oh! THAT TALK! Yeah, my dad gave it to me, too."

TIME TO TALK ABOUT "THE TALK"

When was the first time you learned about how babies are made? How did you feel? (Parents first.)

How have you gotten your best information? How do you know it was accurate?

How would you grade Mom and Dad on THE TALK?

When is the best time to talk about sex education and what in your opinion is the best way to talk to kids? (Kids first.)

If sex is and always has been a fact of life for human beings, ever since the beginning of time, why do we all still giggle when the topic comes up?

37

Savoir Faire

The French have a beautiful word for the art of knowing how to act properly--*savoir faire* (pronounced "sav war farh"). Such an elegant phrase! It makes you want to sit up straight in your seat and fix your hair and tuck in your shirt. Another beautiful French word for good breeding and refined manners is *savoir vivre* (pronounced "sav war vev").

SHALL WE?

1. Have you ever thought why manners are important? What would our world be like if people didn't learn manners and proper behavior and other common codes for conduct?

2. Have you been around people with NO *savoir faire* or zip *savoir vivre?* Describe their behavior. What is the effect of bad and crude manners on others?

3. Did you know that out there in real life, for example, in the business world, job applicants are often judged on their personal manners and table manners, as well as qualification and skills? How come?

38

Sit in Somebody's Chair

READ BEFORE DINNER

You've probably heard of a wise saying that the Indians used:

"To know someone, you must first walk in their shoes."

Tonight let's see how well we know the "someones" in our family. We want to do a little experiment and take that interesting phrase a little further. We suggest that to know someone you must . . .

FIRST SIT IN THEIR CHAIR AT THE DINNER TABLE
WITH THEIR SHOES ON!!!

1. Put the names of all family members in a bowl. Each person draws a name. (If you pick your own name, just put it back and draw again.)

2. Now go sit in the chair that person regularly sits in during dinner. (If you drew Dad's name, go sit in the chair that Dad usually sits in.)

3. AFTER everyone is seated, exchange shoes. If you are sitting in your brother's chair, go get his shoes and put them on--no matter what size. If the shoes are too small, put in just your toes. Got the idea? Keep the shoes on all during dinner because you are getting the "feel" of that person.

DURING DINNER (WITH STRANGE SHOES ON)

Act like that person. No mean things allowed. Just have fun and talk the way that person talks (or doesn't talk), and so on.

AFTER DINNER AND BEFORE DESSERT

In the voice of the person whose shoes you are wearing, describe one thing you really *love to do* and *one of the things you worry about* (in the voice of the person whose shoes you are wearing.) The *real person* is to answer if that is correct or not. *Together,* as a family and in your own voices and with your own shoes on, talk about the experiment.

39

Mama's Gonna Buy You a Diamond Ring

Have you ever heard the lullaby *Hush Little Baby?* Father or mother sings to the baby all the things that he or she will buy for the child: a diamond ring, a looking glass, a mockingbird, a goat, etc. It's a fun song because it points out that if things don't go well-- if the ring turns to brass, if the bird won't sing, if the goat won't go--he or she will find something else to give to the beloved child.

DISCUSS

1. Parents do want to give their children everything to make them happy. Yet, they don't want to spoil them. How do parents distinguish between their child's needs and wants? Children respond first.

2. Everyone think of two things that money can buy that would make them happy.

3. Now, everyone think of two things that money *cannot* buy that would make them happy.

4. Compare some of the things that money can buy with some of the things that money cannot buy. What do you find?

40

More Stop Reminding & Get Creative

Most families are in dire need of fun ways to give reminders to each other. The nagging and fighting is wearing us all out. So AFTER a little success with the "Augean stables," we suggest you try another phrase that will send the message and add a little fun:

HOBSON'S CHOICE

Child (to Mom or Dad): "When you ask me if I want some lima beans, is this a *Hobson's choice?*"

(A Hobson's choice looks like a choice, but in reality there is no choice and you have to accept something whether you like it or not. The term for saying comes from Thomas Hobson, who in 1631 was well known for saying to his customers something like this: "You can take that horse right there or you can take no horse at all." Sound familiar, kids? (Only in our homes, it's usually things like lima beans instead of horses.)

Child (to Mom or Dad): "When you ask me if I want some lima beans, is this a *Hobson's choice* or do I have a real choice?"

Can you think of other examples of "*Hobson's choices*" heard around your house?

41

The Wisdom of the Animals

READ THE FOLLOWING AND PONDER

* "Native Americans saw themselves as participants in a great natural order of life, related in some fundamental manner to every other living species. It was said that each species had a particular knowledge of the universe and specific skills for living in it. . . .

. . . If birds consistently built nests out of certain materials, it meant that they recognized and adjusted to the fact of harsh or mild weather in a certain location. . . .

. . . The building of beaver dams in certain parts of rivers gave information on the depth of water, its purity, the kinds of fish and other water creatures in the locale and the kinds of roots, berries and medicine roots that would be available at that place. . . .

. . . Animal trails were carefully observed by the people because inevitably the game animals would take the shortest and easiest path through mountains, prairies and desert and would not be far from water and edible plants" (Vine Deloria, Jr.).

REACTION

1. Ask family members what they thought about when they listened to that passage.

2. What animals live around our house? What are their names (besides birds, what kind of birds)? What are their habits?

3. How did we do? Do we know a lot about the animals that are our neighbors? Or do we know very little?

Native American Animal Stories, told by Joseph Bruchac (Golden, Colo: Fulcrum, 1992), pp. 9-10.

42

When Actions Speak Too Loudly

A recent TV show featured mothers and daughters who fought a lot. The thirteen-year-old climbed out the window, had sex with her boyfriend, took drugs, drank alcohol, used vulgar language, and lied.

The mother nailed the daughter's room shut, listened in on her conversations, called the girl names, and slapped her.

The psychologist on the show said that if parents and children cannot listen to one another, then they will communicate by doing things to show how they feel.

WHAT DO YOU THINK?

1. What were some of the feelings that the girl and her mother were showing through these actions?

2. Can you think of a time when you acted out your feelings because you couldn't express them?

3. Think of a time when you as parent and child shared in a way that was successful.

4. Does everyone know how to use * "I messages"? **Example: "When you listen to my phone conversations, I feel that you don't trust me."** State the behavior and then the reaction and feeling to it.

Use an "I message" for these situations:

1. Mom wakes you up way too early on Saturday morning. (Someone think of an "I message" tells Mom their reaction and feeling.)

2. Dad prepares a big meal and the kids look at it and say, "Not this again!" (Someone else act as Dad and use an" I message" that respond to the kids' comments.)

*P.E.T., Parent Effectiveness Training, by Thomas Gordon (New York: Wyden, 1970) p. 115.

43

Dreams

One of the glories of being alive is being able to dream. It is a beautiful word. The poets often say things best because they can put a lot of thoughts and feelings into just a few words. Listen to Langston Hughes:

DREAMS

Hold fast to dreams

For if dreams die

Life is a broken-winged bird

That cannot fly.

Hold fast to dreams

For when dreams go

Life is a barren field

Frozen with snow.

1. Sometimes dreams do fall away and sometimes they just change shape. Has this ever happened to you? (Parents first.)

2. William Butler Yeats, the Irish poet, said to "tread softly because you tread on my dreams." (The word tread means to walk.) Are people reluctant to tell others about their dreams? How come?

3. Can you share with each other one of your dreams?

The Collected Poems of Langston Hughes, ed. Arnold Rampersad (New York: Knopf, 1994), p. 32.

44

Do Families Have a Personality?

Preparation: Pen and paper

Think of families that you know. Are they funloving, close, musical, sports fans, religious? Would you say this is their "*personality*"? Do you think different families have different personalities?

BUT . . . is this what makes them tick? What are their underlying beliefs? What do they stand for? What are their values? Another word for beliefs or values is *TESTAMENT*. A *TESTAMENT* is a statement.

OUR FAMILY'S *TESTAMENT*
Let's see if we can say what our family stands for. One person should act as a scribe. To get started, begin with these sentences:

Our family acts on our beliefs by . . .

Our family cherishes . . .

Add as many sentences as you like. When you are finished, hang up the *FAMILY TESTAMENT* on the fridge. During the week, family members can add to it.

45

The Box That Held a Million Graves

Nearly one million soldiers, sailors, medics, nurses and marines have given their lives in the nation's wars to defend our right to cast a vote at the ballot box. (If you like, stop and take a minute of silence in respect for them and think about their sacrifice.)

Were any of these million men and women who gave their lives for democracy related to you? Do you know of any friends or neighbors who lost loved ones while ensuring that people could remain free?

Yet, in the last presidential election, the majority of voters didn't even bother to vote.

A search for answers

1. Is the reason that people don't vote simply a case of laziness?

2. How old do you have to be to vote?

3. Do you know what is required to register to vote? (Some form of identification, like a driver's license) In most states, you can register to vote the *same day* as the election. Is that the the case for your state?

4. What are some good ways to be an informed voter, such as finding out who is running and studying the issues?

5. What do you call a country where there are no elections and people are not permitted to vote or run for office?

6. For children: Have you ever watched an adult vote? Would you like to?

Lasting Thought

"The only thing necessary for the triumph of evil is for good men(women) to do nothing" (Edmund Burke).

46

Spring

Preparation: A pad of paper and a pencil

READ AS SOON AS EVERYONE SITS DOWN

Easter . . . new life . . . eggs . . . the birthing of baby lambs . . . buds on trees . . . peeping flowers . . . the greening of grass . . . playing outside again . . . puddles . . . and more puddles. . . .

Spring . . . calls for a dinner . . . OUTSIDE . . .Tonight . . . everyone pick up their plates and head outdoors--even if you need your coats--set out a blanket or sweep off the patio chair, but eat and smell up (yes, inhale) the GLORIES of Spring.

AFTER DINNER

SPRING . . . the word JUMPS with movement . . . to spring . . . to leap into a new life. Is it time: for a **FAMILY** (dare we say the word?) **Poem** . . . yes, a **family poem!!!**

It's simple, it's fun. Just finish the line. **"SPRING IS . . ."**

TAKE TURNS FINISHING THE LINE (and one person write it all down) . . .

"Spring is . . ." (finish the line with, for example, any color, adjective, description, sentence, foreign names, strings of words), but finish "SPRING IS."

Now **read the FAMILY POEM aloud** again but backwards. Yes, **read it backwards**.

Optional second stanza: "I am Spring when. . . ."(Repeat: write, read frontward and backward) and now HANG IT on the refrigerator door.

Ah, a family of poets.

47

Then . . . in 1776 . . . and Now . . . July 4th.

Preparation: Get a copy of the Declaration of Independence

BEFORE THAT PICNIC, BEFORE THE FIREWORKS, BEFORE THE PARADE, BEFORE ALL THE RED, WHITE, AND BLUE EVENTS TODAY.

Let's take a few minutes at dinner (and it may have to be the night before), but let's take time to *REFLECT* on some of the greatest and highest ideals ever written and sought and aimed for by human beings: **DEMOCRACY!**

But let's make it really personal. Go around the table and have each person tell:

1. What are your favorite lines from the Declaration of Independence? Or favorite story about the writing or signing of the Declaration. (Have a copy out for a day or two for everyone to read. Look in the kids' history books or go to the library and make copies.)

That was then . . . in 1776.

2. And now . . . in the year____ . . . go around and talk about the things you like most about living in the free country of the United States of America.

NOW, GO PARTY . . .

AND

ENJOY THE FEELING OF FREEDOM!!!

48

More Signals & Key Words . . .

THE GRASSHOPPER AND THE ANTS (Adapted from Aesop)

READ THIS STORY AND LISTEN FOR A SIGNAL OR A KEY WORD

One hot summer day a grasshopper was sitting on a blade of grass singing away as he watched a line of ants go by. The ants were busy carrying food to their anthill to store away for the winter. "Hey, ants, why are you working so hard? Sit here in the sun with me and sing and relax a little." But the ants were too busy to join him.

Then winter came and the grasshopper was hungry because he had not put away any food. So the grasshopper went to the ants and asked for some of their food. "Why didn't you put some food away for the winter? You knew you'd be needing it," The ants asked the grasshopper. "I was busy singing," the grasshopper said. So the ants responded, "Well, if you were singing all summer, then you can dance all winter."

Sound familiar?

1. Does this ever happen in your house? Do some people work hard while others "sit and sing?" What are some of the other messages in this story?

2. Share your ideas for a signal word or phrase to use the next time someone acts like the grasshopper.

49

Fame

"Whosoever is energetic, mindful, pure in conduct, discriminating, self-restrained, right-living, vigilant, his [or her] fame steadily increases."*

This selection from *The Dhammapada,* the religion of Buddhism is very interesting for people everywhere.

WHAT DOES IT MEAN?

1. Reread the first part . . . "Whosoever is energetic . . ." Why is it a good thing to be energetic? What is the opposite of energetic? Is that a good way to be?

2. "Whosoever is . . . mindful." What is meant by "mindful"? What is "mindless"? Why is it a good thing to be mindful rather than mindless?

3. "Whosoever is . . . pure in conduct." What does this mean? Is it good to be bad of conduct?

4. "Whosoever is . . . discriminating." Here the words are used in the sense of being able to judge for yourself. Why is it a problem for people when they don't make up their own minds? Give examples.

5. "Whosoever is . . . self-restrained." People who are not self-restrained are people who act impulsively. Give examples trouble caused by acting impulsively.

6. "Whosoever is all these things his [or her] fame steadily increases." Are they talking about "fame" as we know it, like people in the movies, on TV, etc. Could another word for "fame" be "honor" or "reputation"?

Reread the quote with the substituted words: "Whosoever is energetic, mindful, pure in conduct, discriminating, self-restrained, right-living, vigilant, his *honor or reputation* increases."

*Adapted from Walpola Rahula, *What the Buddha Taught* (Grove Press, 1959), pp.125-34.

50

Backyard Adventures

"My Son John" is the story of a rich young boy who lives in a big, expensive house with a big green lawn surrounded by a high fence. John and his brother play there until one day he gets punished and is told to go sit in the backyard on the steps.

All of a sudden, John discovers his backyard! There is no fence and he can see into the alley where there are rusted cars, old junk piled up high, and overgrown bushes. He sees lots of people, too. He sees some people looking for food, others going through the trash and he sees some people begging. Then he hears children laughing. He follows their laughter and finds the children. Some of them are brown and black and white, some are dressed in ragged clothes. Others are splashing around in the muddy water. They wave to him. He waves back and goes to join them. Soon he too is dirty and wet and having a wonderful time.

Then it is time for John to go home. He steps into his backyard and he realizes that the things his family has, the big house, the fenced in front yard--are keeping him from the children he met in his backyard.

HAVE YOU EVER HAD ANY BACKYARD EXPERIENCES?

1. Parents begin with their stories of the times when they realized they had things that others didn't.

2. Who would you meet in your "backyard" if you lost your "front-yard" privileges?

3. What keeps people of different incomes apart?

4. What did John learn in his backyard?

*Adapted from *Love, Love at the End,* by Daniel Berrigan, S.J., (New York: Macmillan, 1971), pp. 7-9.

51

Vacations

What does the word "vacate" mean? What does "intermission" mean? Have you ever thought of **vacation** being any of those things?

List some of the places your family has gone together on a vacation.

1. Go around the table and make a **WISH LIST OF VACATION PLACES**. Everyone tell one or two places that they would love to see, go to, or experience. Someone write down all the ideas.

2. Now put an **X** by the ones that are possible--if not possible this year, maybe someday.

3. Vacations can be far away and for long periods of time **or** vacations can be *day trips*. Make a list of interesting *day trips* to go on together as a family.

4. Vacations can also be *doing something completely different.* For example, the first Saturday of each month could be a day when one person in the family (take turns) has no chores, gets breakfast in bed, or does whatever he or she wants! That's a vacation!!! Brainstorm for ways to make the first Saturday **VACATION DAY!**

52

Applause, Presents & Congratulations

We've finished all the topics!!! Hooray!!! Great job!

IT'S TIME TO PARTY!!! SOMEONE PICK OUT SOME COOL MUSIC . . . SOMEONE ELSE LIGHT THE CANDLES . . . AND EVERYBODY HAVE SOME FUN!!!

No list of questions tonight . . . well, maybe *just one big one.*

Go around the table and ask each person:

Do you think we got to know each other better and have we grown closer from talking together and eating together as a family?

Say no more . . . just enjoy. . . .

applause, applause, applause . . .

. . . to a great family!